D1784993

The RHYME

of the

REDDLEMAN'S

DAUGHTER

The RHYME

of the

REDDLEMAN'S

DAUGHTER

by James Simpson

First published in 2015 as a limited edition artist's book by Parvenu Press

This edition published in the UK by
The Hedgehog Poetry Press
5, Coppack House,
Churchill Avenue
Clevedon
BS21 6QW

www.hedgehogpress.co.uk

ISBN: 978-1-9164806-3-6

Copyright © James Simpson 2019

The right of James Simpson to be identified as the author of this work has been asserted in accordance with the Copyright, Designs and Patents Act 1988.

All rights reserved. No part of this publication may be reproduced, stored in or introduced into a retrieval system, or transmitted in any form, or by any means (electronic, mechanical, photocopying, recording or otherwise) without prior written permissions of the publisher. Any person who does any unauthorised act in relation to this publication may be liable for criminal prosecution and civil claims for damages.

9 8 7 6 5 4 3 2 1

A CIP Catalogue record for this book is available from the British Library.

for Olwen May

THE RHYME

OF THE

REDDLEMAN'S DAUGHTER

IN SEVEN PARTS

I

Wine berry, ta diddle, wagtail, den,
  he counted as he walked;
to the spring of St Catherine
  which bubbles from the chalk.

Yellow flag, buttercup, forget me not,
  he led his horse to grass;
to drink the sharp cold that rippled
  near old Cocking pass.

And there the midges and the bats
  were whirligigging dusk
beneath an ash tree canopy
  where the minnowing stream ran past.

Ragged robin, bittercress,
  rushes black and bull
and the worn flints that lay below
  the water chuckling full.

Underneath a homely ash
  he built a fine campfire;
and a ribbon of smoke and scaddle sparks
  drifted higher and higher.

He unhitched a tin bath from his cart,
  filled it from the spring,
and steaming water from his kettle,
  he lifted and poured it in.

Then he picked his daughter up,
  his lovely poppet dear,
and popped her in the piping bath
  a cloud pond still and clear.

'Too hot', 'too hot' she laughed aloud,
  so he stirred it round and round
and a rust red stain washed from his hands
  as a memory unwound.

And then she spoke, like a bright bell,
  like a cuckoo's voice in May,
as the sun dew lipped its afterglow
  at the compline of the day.

II

'I'll tell a story from my mouth
  of a dream I dreamt Oh daddy dear
and the world it was a sorrow place,
  when child and man had sunken face
and the earth was dust and drear.

From East to West and West to East
  no shred of grass would grow;
and all the trees had been stripped bare
  and the winds had ceased to blow.

Ash and chestnut, elm and beech
  were lifeless standing things
and dry dead twigs were rattling
  like a thousand golden rings.

Every crystal chalk stream
  was a dust dry ridden track;
no sweet sucking from the trout pools
  or beaded otter back.

No beasts that crawl upon the earth,
  no moths or butterflies,
no spiders or slow pulsing worms,
  no birds to mark the skies.

A throng of people gathered
   imploring God on high
but no god was there to hear them,
   he'd left them bye and bye.

Little children cried aloud
   through the stagnant air;
asking why the world was barren,
   like a bone picked bare.

And their mothers and their fathers
   could not look them in the eye;
they'd eaten every living thing
   that could walk, or crawl or fly.

Then it seemed that all the people
   were calling out as one,
a million, million, raw swollen tongues
   clacking at the sun.

III

Who saw where she had come from,
  who knew from where she came,
like a green blade rising
  from the buried grain?

I felt the earth was trembling,
  and like a split hillside,
a giantess stood there,
  with barley straw for her hair
as a turning tide.

She stood alone amongst them,
  a bursting corn sack moon
and her eyes they had a sadness
  a honeysuckle gloom.

Her tears were those of one who loves
  but knows of what will be,
like a willow weeping quietly
  like a wind-blown tree.

She gathered them up gently,
  in ones, and twos and threes
and gnawed their limbs,
  and stuffed them in,
her stump teeth chewed,
  her gristle food,
with a jaunce and weary grin.

IV

A gaunt procession shuffled along,
   man, woman, sunk eyed child,
like a sow devouring her farrow,
   her eyes were wide and wild.

Her work went on; on and on,
   on into the night,
the moon rose in the dead sky
   guttering a torn moth light.

The moon it hung, a plucked out eye,
   and her work went on and on;
her feeding was swift now
   as swallows before a storm.

At last, no tears; her tears were gone
   and now her work was done;
she hugged herself shivering,
   huddled cold and dumb.

Then with her nails she raked her face,
   until she drew blood;
and then she tore her barley hair,
   in ragged clumps
with bits of scalp in clotted lumps,
   until her skull was bare.

And in her grief the giantess
   laid on the earth and died;
no living thing was left there
   but dust and sand and stillborn air;
for age on age the addled air,
   and the rocks beside.

V

Time blinked; and in the distance
  I saw a whirling wind;
far out on the horizon,
  I saw a whirling wind!

And I could hear a little thing
  full hearted like a wren;
deep in the swirling of the storm,
  a droplet diadem.

There somewhere inside the wind
  a ripple in the light;
like a mirage, like water's fire,
  a whirlpool of the night.

Stepping from the spinning winds,
  the twisting sands and dust,
a tiger walked and padded forth,
  singing a dawn chorus.

The tiger padded through the waste
  his shimmering sides a glare,
singing a mournful elegy
  of what had gone before.

VI

Such a song I never heard
  or ever will again;
like the lonely voice of a green plover
  or longed for summer rain.

And then I saw a precious thing
  for where his footprints lay,
grew up some white dead nettle
  like the dawning of the day.

And with his song of sweet lament
  a mourned for long dead choir;
new living things sprung from the earth,
  a birch bark kindling fire.

I saw the place where the roebuck lay,
  I heard the vixen's cry;
and I marked a flock of jackdaws
  across the southern sky.

Yellowhammer, woodlark,
  grey partridge and quail,
were calling from the grasses
  the cocksfoot and foxtail.

The eel within the spring pool
  curled in its bed of leaves;
and silver-washed fritillaries
  gilded the woodland eaves.

And with his song of utmost joy,
  hazels grew gold and green;
as a heron misted northwards
  over dew cobwebbed hornbeams.

VII

And I awoke on the high blown down
   with swallows above my head
and I did not know if these things had been
   or were to come instead.

And I awoke not knowing,
   if the tiger would sing once more;
if he would call us back again
   as he had done before.'

There under the homely ash
   the Reddleman's daughter yawned;
'Have I dreamed a dream, oh Daddy dear,
   of how the world was born?'

He stirred the dying embers,
   while the hoolets screeched and knelled,
as his daughter turned to sleeping
   sound as a clucket bell.

By the last of the fire,
   he wondered at what was said;
as its tiver glow passed from her face
   and he carried her to bed.

Wine berry, ta diddle, wagtail, den
   he counted as he walked;
leading his horse, up the scarp slope bare,
   onto the hills of chalk.

Acknowledgements

My grateful thanks go to the editor of *The London Magazine* who has published several sections of *The Rhyme of the Reddleman's Daughter*, including parts V-VII in the 2016 Christmas issue. A version of the poem was also published as an artist's book with Parvenu Press in 2015.